GW01388412

Elementary
Audio-Typing
Second Edition

Barbara Colley

Head of Business Studies
Parsloes Manor Comprehensive School

McGRAW-HILL BOOK COMPANY
London • New York • St Louis • San Francisco
Auckland • Bogotá • Guatemala • Hamburg • Lisbon
Madrid • Mexico • Montreal • New Delhi • Panama
Paris • San Juan • São Paulo • Singapore • Sydney
Tokyo • Toronto

Published by
McGRAW-HILL Book Company (UK) Limited
Shoppenhangers Road, Maidenhead, Berkshire, England
TEL: 0628 23423 FAX: 0628 35895

British Library Cataloguing in Publication Data

Colley, Barbara, *1950–*
    Elementary audio – typing. - 2nd ed
    1. Audio – typing
    I. Title
    652.3

    ISBN 0–07–707271–5

Library of Congress Cataloging-in-Publication Data

Colley, Barbara.
    Elementary audio-typing / Barbara Colley. —2nd ed.
        p.   cm.
    ISBN 0–07–707271–5 : £4.50
    1. Typewriting. 2. Dictation (Office practice)   I. Title.
    Z49.C67 1990
    652.3—dc20   89–13842
                                                  CIP

Typeset by Electronic Images, Cambridge
Printed and bound in Great Britain by The Information Press, Oxford

CONTENTS

Unit 8   Advanced work:
         Letter with address dictated   Estimating paper size
         (Task 35)
         List with numbered points   Instructions being given
         (Task 36)   during dictation
         Composition – reply to a letter   Replying to a letter from
         (Task 37)   notes that have been dictated
         Letter requiring several copies   "Enc" is required by the
         (Task 38)   typist
         Report on a software package   Shoulder headings and
         (Task 39)   instructions given during
                                            dictation

INTRODUCTION

When to introduce audio-typing

There are two approaches to audio training.
   (1) The "end-on" approach, where the students are almost
      at the end of their training and are already
      competent typists. Audio-typing is then introduced
      intensively over a short period of time.
   (2) The "integrated" approach, where audio-typing is part
      of the student's overall training. The students
      spend some time on audio-typing each week once the
      keyboard has been completed and their knowledge of
      the machine is sufficient to allow the new skill of
      audio to be introduced. This audio training quite
      often has to be allowed for within the time allocated
      for typewriting and can be done on a rota system.
   The method used will depend upon personal preferences,
the teaching situation and the ability of the students.
   If only a few audio machines are available, audio
training can still be included. The training would need to
begin as early as possible to allow for a rota system,
granting sufficient time for each student to cover the
course.
   Whatever method is used, it must be remembered that each
type of display must be taught in typewriting lessons *before*
being introduced in audio-typing. Audio-typing is an
additional skill and cannot replace typewriting lessons.

Special features of the course

The "Instructions" section will cover the recording and
dubbing of the material on to tape or cassette. The book is
prepared in such a way that teachers can quickly and easily
prepare their own tapes, and, if required, make alterations.
For example, it may be preferable in the "letter" sections
to use place names more familiar to the students. This can
be done simply by altering names and addresses as the
material is dictated. It is quite deliberately a short,
step-by-step course and is structured so that it can be used
in any teaching situation.
   Unit 1 begins with a listening exercise for the students.
This is to allow them to get the feel of the headset, adjust
the volume and generally gain confidence in their use of the
machine.
   Unit 8 includes examples of more advanced work. These
can be used as a guide for the teacher, so that similar
material can be presented to the students after completion
of the course.
   Students will only begin typing when they hear THIS IS
THE TASK ... and will stop typing when they hear END OF
TASK. They will continue to listen until they hear END OF
DICTATION and the tape will then be at the correct point for

1

the next section of work. The teacher must give the *starting* point at the end of each task. It is important to note this number.

Prerequisites

It is generally thought that a typewriting speed of approximately 25 wpm is the minimum requirement before audio training can begin. The students will, at that stage of their training, be confident in their basic typewriting skills, before the additional skill of audio-typing is introduced. Because of the structure of this course, audio could be introduced immediately the keyboard has been completed.

Rate of progress

Each student *must* have control of his or her own machine as it will be found that the rate of progress will vary considerably from student to student. Therefore, within a short space of time the students will be working on different units during the same lesson. This is to be expected. The course has been prepared to allow for this by providing model answers as well as a reference section. However, in some units preliminary work with the students will be necessary. This was deliberate. Although the class will be working very largely as individuals during their audio training, it is useful to bring them together occasionally as a class. It is suggested that when some of the students are about to begin a unit that contains a set list of difficult words, or a particularly difficult section of the work, this work should be done with the class as a whole.

Students on full-time secretarial courses would benefit by working through this course and then moving on to past examination papers at the relevant level.

Integration

The course will give the students a sound basic training in audio-typing. At the same time it will reinforce their knowledge of typewriting on such simple topics as styles of paragraphs and the layout of A4 and A5 letters, memos and envelopes. Their knowledge of punctuation should improve considerably.

The word "drills" in the reference section can be included as a regular part of the audio lesson or can be used for extra work or homework.

Correction of errors

Students *must* check their work from the model answers but should *never* retype work from their corrected copy or from

the model answers. Students must retype tasks by using the
tape. The model answers must be used for correction only.
Each time the student finishes a section of work, he or she
is instructed to check it from the model answer, placing a
circle around each error. The work should then be shown to
the teacher. When the teacher is satisfied, the student
completes the record sheet and continues with the next
section. In audio-typing record sheets are essential.
These will be discussed in the "Instructions" section.

INSTRUCTIONS FOR THE TEACHER

Recording

(1) The "master" or original tape

The material to be dictated is marked by a black line on the left margin and is <u>word for word</u> what should be dictated.

The instructions to the students should be dictated in a normal speaking voice at a fairly fast pace. When dictating the actual tasks, an average speed of 80 wpm is recommended. It is *very important* that the natural inflexions of the voice are retained. <u>Shorthand-style dictation is a handicap to the audio-typist</u>. Do not become a slave to the stop-watch when dictating. Dictate for meaning rather than speed. The more lengthy pieces of dictation have been counted in 40s <u>as a guide only</u>. Always take into account the difficulty of the task but remember that dictating too slowly destroys the meaning, and, therefore, the student's comprehension of the passage.

When dictating, make a note at the beginning of each task of the point on the scale at which the dictation begins. This is included in the instructions to students at the end of each task. It will enable them to find quickly the correct tape and the exact position of the piece they are to type. Both the tapes and their containers should be numbered. Remember to number each side.

Towards the end of the course, when the students have become familiar with the techniques required in audio-typing, different voices should be used for recording.

(2) Dubbing

This involves making as many copies as are needed from the "master".

A complete audio system will include dubbing facilities. If in any doubt about how this equipment works, an audio engineer should be asked to assist with the dubbing of the first set of tapes. Dubbing can be a time-consuming task. One way of dealing with this (depending on the students) is to set up the audio machines just before the lunch break, and ask each student to insert a cassette or tape, making sure that the indicator in on "0", and that the correct side is being used. Make sure that the dubbing leads are connected. Insert the "master", operate the control panel, and the tape will be dubbed during the lunch-hour.

A dubbing machine is available that will, in one operation, duplicate both sides of the "master" in five minutes. This machine is particularly convenient when space or time are restricted. The machine is simple to operate, as well as being light to carry.

Record of work

This is *essential* in audio-typing. The students will be working largely on their own and will need to feel that a record of their work is being kept. Records are also useful in assisting the teacher in monitoring the work of the class. If completed by the student at the end of each session, there will be no loss of time at the beginning of the next session. The record sheet (as given on page 76) should be duplicated for use by both teacher and students. The students should keep their own record sheets with their audio work; a teacher's copy can be kept as a check.

Handouts

There are two sections containing business letters. At this stage a handout giving the names and addresses for each letter should be duplicated by the teacher and given to the student. If it is felt advisable to change the addresses, this can be done simply by altering the place names contained in the actual dictation, to correspond with those given on the handout.

Preliminary work

Most units contain "Notes to the Teacher". These give general information on punctuation and dictation conventions as well as words that might cause spelling difficulties. It may be advisable to give some preliminary work on the topics contained in each unit. It can help to bring the class together occasionally by doing some preliminary work with the whole class as soon as some of the students are ready to begin a particular unit. At the discretion of the teacher, extra work can be given on formal English.

The first lesson

All machines should be set up ready for use, complete with headset and foot pedal, with a tape inserted. The teacher should demonstrate the operation of the foot pedal to play and to rewind, and explain the counter indicator and the volume control. The students can then begin right away with the listening exercise. At the end of the lesson, allow ample time for instruction on the rewinding of the tape, completion of the record sheet if any tasks were produced, and for the students to pack away the equipment. Ask the students to rewind their tapes ready for use by the next class. This is very important.

The second lesson

At the beginning of the next lesson the class should be instructed in the assembling of the equipment. The whole class should perform each operation at the same time.

Summary of introduction to equipment

The following points should be explained and demonstrated.

Lesson 1:	Use of headset
	Operation of foot pedal (1) Start
	(2) Stop
	(3) Rewind
	(correct position of foot)
	Volume control
	Counter indicator
End of Lesson 1:	Instruction on rewinding the tape
	How to pack equipment away
Lesson 2:	Assembling the equipment

Model answers

Students must use these in the correct way. The business letters, envelopes and memos are shown in the style of open punctuation. Full punctuation can be accepted. Only the essential commas are shown. If students insert other commas, these need not necessarily be incorrect.

DICTATION MATERIAL AND NOTES TO THE TEACHER

Unit 1

Notes to the teacher

This is a listening exercise followed by simple short sentences for typing.

Listening exercise as for dictation on to cassette.

This is unit 1 of your audio-typing course

This is probably the first time you have listened to a voice through a headset and I shall talk to you for a short time before you actually begin work, to help you to become used to this and to explain some of the most important points regarding audio-typing. Adjust the volume of your machine if necessary.

Good audio-typists type continuously. They stop the audio machine when they wish but continue typing. This is a skill which will come with practice.

During your audio-typing lessons we will begin with simple sentences so that you can get used to the operation of the audio machine and we will then progress to paragraphs, letters and memos so that by the end of your course you will be an efficient audio-typist.

It is important that you understand what you are typing and, therefore, when you are audio-typing, you *must* listen for meaning. If what you hear does not make sense, play that part again until the meaning *does* become clear. When audio-typing, always have a dictionary at your side and look up spellings of which you are unsure.

Your aim when audio-typing is to type direct from the spoken word, correcting your typing errors as you go along. If your teacher asks you to do a particular exercise again, do not copy it from what you have previously typed. Use your audio machine.

In typewriting lessons you have kept your eyes on the copy when typing. Now that you are going to be typing from the spoken word and do not have to look at the copy, do not be tempted to look at your fingers. Keep your eyes on the paper in your machine or straight ahead of you.

Now put a sheet of A4 paper into your machine and set your left-hand margin at 25 mm (one inch). You will not need to set your right-hand margin at this stage. I am going to dictate ten short, simple sentences. Because the skilled audio-typist listens to quite a long piece of dictation before needing to stop the machine, we are going to train you to do this. So you must listen to the whole sentence before you begin to type it.

The end of each task will be indicated by the words END OF TASK. Then listen for instructions until you hear END OF DICTATION. Your tape will then be in position for the next task.

Here are the instructions for this task.

Each sentence is to begin on a fresh line, so as soon as you have finished typing one sentence, press return, start your audio machine and listen to the next sentence. Then type it. Continue in this way until you have typed all the sentences. Use double-line spacing. Do not correct any typing errors at the moment. Concentrate on getting used to the new skill of audio-typing. We will concern ourselves with typing errors a little later on.

The end of a sentence will be indicated by the words FULL STOP or QUESTION MARK.

Are you ready for the sentences?

This is task 1

Thank you for your letter (*full stop*)
I hope you will come (*full stop*)
They say it is easy (*full stop*)
We agree with them (*full stop*)
The prices are very low (*full stop*)
Would you agree with that (*question mark*)
We shall see you tomorrow (*full stop*)
They seem to have problems (*full stop*)
Is that very common (*question mark*)
I think it is common (*full stop*)

END OF TASK

The dictation started at point (   ) on your indicator scale. Make a note of this number. Using the model answers, check your work carefully. Place a circle around any mistake. Show the work to your teacher. If it is satisfactory, you may go on to the next section. Remember to fill in your record sheet. If you are asked to do it again,

    1   rewind the tape to the point where the dictation began
    2   type from the tape

Do not copy your typing.

END OF DICTATION

This time the ten sentences are going to be just a little longer. Again use double-line spacing and A4 paper. Begin each sentence on a fresh line, so press return as soon as you have typed each sentence, and remember to listen to the whole sentence before beginning to type it. Now that you are a little more familiar with what you have to do, I expect you to correct your errors as you go along.
Are you ready for the sentences?

8

This is task 2
Thank you for your letter of yesterday (*full stop*)
I hope you will come to the factory (*full stop*)
They say it is easy to find (*full stop*)
We agree with them that it is (*full stop*)
We feel the prices are very low (*full stop*)
Would you agree that they are (*question mark*)
We shall see you tomorrow if you wish (*full stop*)
They seem to have problems just now (*full stop*)
Do you think that it is common (*question mark*)
I do think it is quite common (*full stop*)

END OF TASK

The dictation started at point ( ) on your indicator scale.
Check your work from the model answers and show your work to
the teacher. If it is satisfactory, you may go on to the
next section. Complete your record sheet. If you have to
do the section again, remember to rewind the tape and type
from that. It is the only way you can expect to become a
good audio-typist.

END OF DICTATION

Notes to the teacher

The next section includes some words that may cause
difficulties, depending upon the ability of the students.
Listed here are the most difficult words and it is suggested
that a lesson be given dealing with these spellings,
depending on the needs of the students.

RECEIVE	COMPLETELY	ENCLOSE	SUCCESSFUL	ACCOUNT
ATTENDED	TRANSFER	STATEMENT	CHEQUE	USEFUL

Pay particular attention to words that sound similar to
others.

I will now dictate ten short sentences containing the words
you have just dealt with. Again use A4 paper, double-line
spacing and a left-hand margin of 25 mm (1 inch). Begin each
sentence on a fresh line, remembering to listen to the whole
of the sentence before you begin to type. Correct your
errors as you go along.
Are you ready?

This is task 3
I am happy to enclose a bank statement (*full stop*)
The meeting I have attended was successful (*full stop*)
We were able to transfer a large sum of money (*full stop*)
When shall I receive your cheque in payment (*question mark*)
The bank is expecting to receive a cheque (*full stop*)
The inspector was completely satisfied with the report (*full
   stop*)

9

I hope you were successful in your recent test (*full stop*)
We shall be happy to come to the meeting tomorrow (*full stop*)
Do you have a bank account (*question mark*)
I hope you found the talk useful (*full stop*)

END OF TASK

The dictation began at point ( ) on the indicator scale.
Check your work from the model answers, placing a circle
around each error. Then show your work to your teacher.

END OF DICTATION

In the next section there will be ten longer sentences based
on the ones you have just typed. Use A4 paper, and the same
margin and line-spacing as before. Listen to the whole
sentence before beginning to type it. If you cannot
remember it, listen to the whole sentence again before
beginning to type.
Are you ready?

This is task 4

I am happy to enclose a bank statement giving full details (*full stop*)
The meeting I have attended was successful and useful (*full stop*)
We were able to transfer a large sum of money to your account (*full stop*)
When shall I receive your cheque in payment of the goods (*question mark*)
The bank is expecting to receive a cheque from you soon (*full stop*)
The inspector was completely satisfied with the report given to him (*full stop*)
I hope the recent tests proved to be successful (*full stop*)
We shall be happy to meet you for a talk tomorrow (*full stop*)
Do you have a cheque book and a statement (*question mark*)
I hope you found the talk completely to your satisfaction (*full stop*)

END OF TASK

The dictation began at point ( ) on the indicator scale.
Check your work from the model answers, placing a circle
around each error. Show your work to your teacher.

END OF DICTATION

10

Unit 2

This is unit 2

Follow the same instructions as for Unit 1 for all tasks.
Are you ready?

This is task 5

Many thanks for your letter of yesterday (*full stop*)
I was hoping we could go to the coast (*full stop*)
If the weather remains good we shall go (*full stop*)
We have several friends who live there (*full stop*)
Shall we drive there or go on the train (*question mark*)
Perhaps we can stay with our friends (*full stop*)
If not we can stay at a local hotel (*full stop*)
The rates they charge are very reasonable (*full stop*)

                                                    END OF TASK

The dictation began at point ( ) on your indicator scale.
As usual check your work from the model answers, placing a
circle around each error. Show the work to your teacher.
If it is satisfactory, complete your record sheet and go on
to the next section. If it is necessary to repeat the
section, remember to use the tape.

                                                    END OF DICTATION

Notes to the teacher

The next section contains sentences in which dashes,
exclamation marks and brackets will be used.

So far the only punctuation you have used has been the full-
stop and the question mark. But there are many more signs,
and now we will use the dash, exclamation mark and bracket.
All of these will be dictated. Some of the sentences that
follow are quite long. Listen to the whole sentence before
beginning to type it. If necessary, listen to the sentence
more than once until the meaning becomes quite clear. Pay
special attention to the new punctuation signs.
    The *dash* is used to show additional information in a
sentence and calls special attention to that information.
    You will hear:
"The new forms (*dash*) the green ones (*dash*) are now being
used (*full stop*)" Leave one space before and after the dash.

11

This is task 6 part A

The new forms (*dash*) the green ones (*dash*) are now being
used (*full stop*)
Our directors (*dash*) there are three (*dash*) have given their
permission (*full stop*)
Do come to see us (*dash*) you are always welcome (*full stop*)
Last week (*dash*) on Wednesday (*dash*) he resigned (*full stop*)
(*Leave one extra line space*)

END OF TASK

The *exclamation mark* usually indicates that something has
been said very strongly, like an order; or it shows surprise.
    You will hear:
"We are the greatest (*exclamation mark*)"

This is task 6 part B

We are the greatest (*exclamation mark*)
Go abroad this year (*exclamation mark*)
Hurry up or we shall be late (*exclamation mark*)
(*Leave one extra line space*)

END OF TASK

The *bracket* is also called a parenthesis. Like the dash, it
shows additional information.
    You will hear:
"You will be allowed three days (*open brackets*) the maximum
(*close brackets*) for travel (*full stop*)"
    Do not leave a space between the brackets and the first
word, and between the last word and the bracket.

This is task 6 part C

You will be allowed three days (*open brackets*) the maximum
(*close brackets*) for travel (*full stop*)
The girl (*open brackets*) the young one (*close brackets*)
came home (*full stop*)

END OF TASK

The dictation began at point ( ) on your indicator scale.
Check your work, using the model answers. Circle each error
and show the work to your teacher. If the teacher agrees,
go on to the next section, completing your record sheet. Do
the section again if asked to.

END OF DICTATION

Notes to the teacher

The next sentences contain some words that your students may
find a little difficult. The words are listed below.

ACCOMMODATE ACCOMMODATION ALL RIGHT CERTAIN EXCELLENT
EXTREMELY   FAMILIAR   HEIGHT   VACANT   IMPORTANT

Task 8 introduces the "comma".
Use A4 paper and follow all the instructions previously
given.
Are you ready for the sentences?

This is task 7

It is hoped to be able to accommodate you (*full stop*)
The hotel manager was certain he had vacant accommodation
    (*full stop*)
Our neighbour was very good to us (*full stop*)
The meeting is extremely important to them (*full stop*)
They asked if you were all right (*full stop*)
Do you know the height of the building (*question mark*)
You will need to be familiar with these words (*full stop*)
The results of the tests (*open brackets*) the latest (*close
    brackets*) were excellent (*full stop*)
The doctor said he was completely recovered (*full stop*)

                                            END OF TASK

The dictation began at point ( ) on the indicator scale.
The instructions for checking your work will not be given to
you from now on, but you must remember to carry them out.

                                        END OF DICTATION

We will now begin to use the comma.
    In audio-typing, commas will *not* be dictated, so you must
think about when to use them. It is usually only necessary
to insert the most essential ones. Study this in the
"reference" section. It is important that you read this and
fully understand it before going any further.
    I will explain the most important uses and give two
examples of each. You should type the examples.
    Commas are used to separate lists of items but are not
placed before the word "and".
TYPE THE EXAMPLES:
    The girl went shopping to buy cheese, butter, eggs and
    tomatoes (*full stop*)
    Red, yellow, green and blue (*full stop*)

    Commas are used to separate words or phrases used as an
explanation.
TYPE THE EXAMPLES:
    Miss Jones, a fine person, was given the job (*full stop*)

13

The manager, Mr Thomas, was asked to give a lecture (*full stop*)
Notice that the name (Mr Thomas) explains who the manager is.

Commas are used to separate a number of words that are used to describe something.
TYPE THE EXAMPLES:
The girl was quiet, efficient, pleasant and an asset to the firm (*full stop*)
She was an attractive, tall girl (*full stop*)

Show this work to your teacher before going any further.
Are you ready for the sentences?

This is task 8
The manager feels that, by Friday, a decision must be made (*full stop*)
If you are to obtain a job, you should be bright, cheerful and dedicated (*full stop*)
You cannot expect to get a cheque, cash and a gift (*full stop*)
I hope the boy, John, will be happy in his work (*full stop*)
The accommodation was reasonably priced, very comfortable and warm (*full stop*)
The audience was extremely happy and cheered loudly (*full stop*)

END OF TASK

The dictation began at point ( ) on the indicator scale.

END OF DICTATION

In the following sentences, some of the difficult words will be spelled out.
You will also be expected to type the colon, semi-colon and solidus, all of which will be dictated. The solidus will be dictated as "oblique". Listen carefully for where you think the commas should be placed.
Are you ready?

This is task 9
I am going on Monday (*colon*) Jim is coming too (T-O-O) (*full stop*)
Mr Shephard (S-H-E-P-H-A-R-D) lives in Leicester (L-E-I-C-E-S-T-E-R) (*full stop*)
It rained yesterday (*semi-colon*) it rained again this morning (*full stop*)
The switch was on (*oblique*) off (*full stop*)
Money owed to someone else is called a liability (L-I-A-B-I-L-I-T-Y) (*full stop*)
One is white (*semi-colon*) the other is black (*full stop*)
These are valuable stones (*colon*) emerald, diamond and sapphire (S-A-P-P-H-I-R-E) (*full stop*)

END OF TASK

14

The dictation began at point ( ) on the indicator scale.
Check your work carefully.

END OF DICTATION

Unit 3

Notes to the teacher

The students may find it difficult to type continuously and may be tempted to play a section and listen to it, then type it and listen to the next section, type it, etc. This is not the correct way to audio-type. Help and encouragement may be needed at this stage. This is the first time students will be called upon to audio-type from continuous matter and it may help to discuss the skill briefly before the students listen to the instructions. Each paragraph in this unit is "counted" as a separate piece.

This is unit 3

So far in your audio-typing course, you have typed sentences and your instructions have been to listen to, and remember, the whole sentence before beginning to type. This has helped you to learn to listen closely to what is being dictated. We are now going to type paragraphs. Obviously you will not be able to listen to, and remember, the whole paragraph before beginning to type. Start your audio-machine and listen to as much as you can remember. Stop your audio-machine and begin to type what you have just heard. Before you finish typing that section, start your audio-machine again and listen to the next piece of dictation while you are still typing the first section. Then, as soon as you have typed the first section of dictation, you can go straight on to the next piece that you have just listened to. Do not play any more than you can remember. Then continue typing. In this way, you are typing almost continuously and listening, occasionally, to the dictation without typing. This will probably be difficult to do at first but this is how an efficient audio-typist works. Replay this piece if it is not clear to you.
   Now let us try some simple *blocked* paragraphs. Use A4 paper, single-line spacing and a 25 mm (one inch) margin on each side of the paper. This will be the first time you have had to use your right-hand margin and so you must listen for the bell if using a typewriter, and decide when to return the carriage. Each new paragraph will be indicated by the word "paragraph".
Are you ready for the paragraphs?

This is task 10

When you leave school and start work, you will probably need a bank account (*full stop*) There are two main types of account (*dash*) current and deposit (*full stop*) A current

16

account is one into which cheques are paid (*full stop*) You
are given a cheque book (*full stop*, *paragraph*)//
If you found that you could afford to save some money, you
could open a deposit account (*full stop*) You are paid
interest on the money you put into a deposit account (*full
stop*, *open brackets*) It is a useful way of saving money
(*full stop*, *close brackets*, *paragraph*)
Banks provide many services for their customers (*full stop*)
If you decide to go abroad for your holiday, the bank will
provide you with currency (*full stop*) They can also help
with insurance, loans and many other things (*full stop*)

                                              END OF TASK

The dictation began at point ( ) on the indicator scale.

                                           END OF DICTATION

We will now type some slightly longer *block* paragraphs. Use
A4 paper, single-line spacing, a 25 mm (one inch) margin on
each side and do try to audio-type correctly by typing as
continuously as you can.
Are you ready for the paragraphs?

This is task 11

Why do people diet (*question mark*) People diet because they
think they are too plump or because they are overweight
(*full stop*) The extent to which you diet is very important
(*dash*) it could be dangerous (*dash*) be careful (*exclamation
mark*) If you are very overweight, a visit // to your doctor
might be helpful (*full stop*, *paragraph*)
Do you ever look back at your past (*question mark*) If you
do, have you realised just how much you have changed
(*question mark*) Your hair may be longer or shorter and you
may have gained or lost weight (*full stop*) Your whole
pattern of life // may have altered considerably (*full stop*)
The things you used to enjoy doing, now hold no pleasure for
you and your tastes in food and music may have changed
greatly (*full stop*, *paragraph*)
Is owning a car an advantage or a disadvantage (*question
mark*) It has one important advantage and that is that it
enables you to travel without having to rely on public
transport or your feet (*full stop*) Although it is expensive
nowadays to run // a car, it is pleasant to travel in the
comfort of your own transport (*full stop*) Perhaps the
biggest disadvantage is the number of accidents occurring on
the roads (*full stop*)

                                              END OF TASK

The dictation began at point ( ) on the indicator scale.

                                           END OF DICTATION

                                                        17

Notes to the teacher

The following paragraphs contain some words that may cause problems. The words are listed below.

DISCUSSED   MINUTES   NECESSARY   BUSINESS   COMMITTEE
OCCASIONALLY   OMITTED   ALTERED   SECRETARY   ARGUMENTS

This section will require the use of the apostrophe. This will not be dictated to the students and, therefore, their knowledge of the use of the apostrophe will need to be sound. (See the "Reference" section)

You are now going to use the apostrophe. Turn to the "Reference" section for some help. When you think you understand this work, type these four sentences.
I carried the lady's bag (*full stop*)
The dog shook its paw (*full stop*)
It's a beautiful day (*full stop*)
The man's coat was wet (*full stop*)

There will now follow some paragraphs in which you will need to use the apostrophe. Use A4 paper, single-line spacing, a 25 mm (one inch) margin on each side and type these paragraphs in the blocked style. Note that inverted commas are dictated and typed in the same way as brackets. Are you ready for the paragraphs?

This is task 12
When you obtain a job as a secretary, it is quite likely that you will be asked to take the minutes of a meeting (*full stop*) These provide a very necessary record of the important points discussed at the meeting (*full stop*) You will // take down, in note form, details of the decisions reached and also the exact wording of every resolution passed (*full stop*) Nothing of importance must be omitted (*full stop, paragraph*)
The committee's decisions must be recorded in the minutes and the secretary must ensure that she notes all the arguments for and against major decisions (*full stop*) Occasionally a mistake may be found in the minutes and this should be corrected before // the minutes are signed (*full stop*) Once they have been signed, they should not be altered in any way (*full stop, paragraph*)
When typing the minutes, they must be recorded in the correct order (*full stop*) It is usual to begin with details such as time and date of meeting, followed by names of those people present with the chairman's name first on the // list (*full stop*) Then the minutes of the last meeting are read and any matters arising from the minutes are discussed (*full stop*) After this, the general business is dealt with and this is followed by an item called (*open quotes*) any other business (*close quotes, full stop*)

END OF TASK

18

The dictation began at point (   ) on the indicator scale.

END OF DICTATION

.

Unit 4

Notes to the teacher

The hyphen will be dictated as "hyphen". The students are going to be asked to type the paragraphs in *indented* style.

This is unit 4

You should now be typing almost continuously.
　　We will now begin using the hyphen – it will be dictated for you as "hyphen". Do not leave a space on either side of it. You will also need to use a hyphen if it is necessary to divide words at the end of your typing line.
　　Use A4 paper, a 25mm (one inch) margin on either side, and set your tab stop for indented paragraphs. Use single-line spacing. Make sure you have a dictionary, as you may need to use it. If you are in any doubt about the spelling of a word, look it up. Remember to audio-type correctly.
Are you ready for the paragraphs?

This is task 13

Thank you for your letter of 21 June, enquiring about our new line in pine kitchen furniture (*full stop*) We hope that the following information will help you (*full stop, paragraph*) We manufacture pine furniture such as tables with matching chairs as well as kitchen // cabinets (*full stop*) In addition we manufacture matching kitchen utensils such as table (*hyphen*) mats, fruit (*hyphen*) salad bowls and trays (*full stop, paragraph*)
Enclosed is a table showing the prices of our equipment and the addresses of stores which stock our goods (*full stop, paragraph*)
If there is any further information // you need, please do not hesitate to contact us again (*full stop*)

                                                        END OF TASK

The dictation began at point (　　) on the indicator scale.

                                                        END OF DICTATION

The following paragraphs are about visiting Holland. Listen carefully for place names and months of the year as well as commas.
　　Use A4 paper, a 25mm (one inch) margin on either side and single-line spacing. Type *indented* paragraphs – set the necessary tab stop.
Are you ready?

20

This is task 14

The best time for the tourist to visit Holland is during these three months (*colon*) June, July and August (*full stop*) It is mild and there is plenty of sunshine (*full stop*) The weather's often good in September, but anyone going outside the summer season // should choose the Spring months (*open brackets*) April and May (*close brackets*), when the bulb fields are in flower (*full stop, paragraph*)
There are a number of ways of getting to Holland (*full stop*) It is possible to go from London by rail or by road (*dash*) both routes require // the use of a ferry (*full stop*) There are direct air services from London to Amsterdam and Rotterdam, and from Manchester to Amsterdam (*full stop, paragraph*)
The famous Dutch (*open quotes*) clogs (*close quotes*) are on sale everywhere and are still in everyday use (*full stop*) Women in national dress can // be seen in the villages, especially on Sundays (*full stop*) It is impossible to be in Holland for more than a brief spell without noticing how fond of music and singing the Dutch are (*full stop*) As likely as not, the quiet of an // evening stroll in a small town will be interrupted by the strains of the local band at practice (*full stop*)

                                                    END OF TASK

The dictation began at point ( ) on the indicator scale.

                                                    END OF DICTATION

Initial capitals will sometimes be dictated for you. When you hear a name or a month of the year dictated, you know that these *must* have a capital letter and, therefore, these will not be dictated. You will use your judgement. However, if you are required to use a capital letter anywhere else, it will be dictated for you. If you are required to put a capital letter to just one word, you will hear the instruction "initial capital" and then the word will be dictated. "Initial capital" means that the first letter of the word will be a capital and the rest of the word will be in lower case. If you are required to begin several words, each with a capital letter, you will hear the instruction "initial capitals" followed by the words.
TYPE THESE EXAMPLES:
    The (*initial capitals*) Deputy Sales Manager arrived at noon (*full stop*)
    We saw the (*initial capital*) Tower in the distance (*full stop*)
    The following paragraph will include initial capitals.
Use A4 paper, a 25 mm (one inch) margin on either side and type the paragraphs in the blocked style. Use double-line spacing.
Are you ready?

This is task 15 part A
The (*initial capitals*) Managing Director asked everyone to
be in the (*initial capitals*) Board Room in good time for the
meeting (*full stop*) He wished to discuss some proposed major
changes in the firm's policy (*full stop*) The (*initial
capitals*) Annual General Meeting was to take place on Friday
next and a decision would need to be taken before then (*full
stop*)

END OF TASK

The following paragraph contains sums of money. These will
be dictated as, for example, "pound sign three point seven
five" or "pound sign oh point six five".

This is task 15 part B
At present the subscription to the (*initial capitals*) Sports
Club is (*pound sign*) eight point two five (*full stop*) It was
proposed that this should be increased to (*pound sign*) ten
point seven five per year (*full stop*) The increase of (*pound
sign*) two point five oh would help to cover the costs of
better facilities (*full stop*)

END OF TASK

The following paragraph refers to the time of the day and
this must be typed in the style of the 24-hour clock. This
will be dictated as it is spoken, e.g. "fifteen hundred
hours", "oh seven twenty hours".

This is task 15 part C
The meeting was due to begin at fourteen hundred hours but
it had to be delayed in order that the (*initial capital*)
Chairman had time to travel from Cardiff to attend the
meeting (*full stop*) At sixteen thirty hours the meeting
began and did not finish until eighteen hundred hours (*full
stop, paragraph*)
The girl had to attend the offices of Smith & Freeman
Limited for an interview at oh nine hundred hours (*full
stop*) Owing to a bus strike, however, she was unable to go
for the interview (*full stop*) She did not know what to do so
she did nothing (*dash*) except go back home (*full stop*) What
should she have done (*question mark*) She should have
telephoned the firm to offer an explanation (*dash*) she could
have asked for another appointment (*full stop*)

END OF TASK

The dictation began at point ( ) on the indicator scale.

END OF DICTATION

22

Notes to the teacher

The following paragraphs form one passage which contains both main headings and side headings. Students will be required to underscore words.

We will now type headings. See the "Reference" section first. Remember that instructions for headings will come before the heading.

When words in a sentence need to be underscored, this instruction will normally come after the dictation of the words to be underscored, for example, "This week's edition of the Mail (*underscore Mail*)."

Use a fresh sheet of A4 paper, single-line spacing, 25mm (one inch) margins on either side and blocked paragraphs. All the dictation is going to form one piece of work under the heading "Terms used in selling".
Are you ready?

This is task 16
(*centred heading, closed capitals, underscored*)   TERMS USED IN SELLING
(*shoulder heading, initial capitals, underscored*) Monthly Credit
Goods are paid for at the end of the month (*full stop*)
Often a cash discount is then allowed (*full stop, paragraph*)
(*shoulder heading, initial capitals, underscored*) Trade Discount
An allowance, usually called a percentage, is // given to enable the wholesaler or retailer to make a profit (*full stop*) It is also given to encourage bulk buying (*underscore bulk buying*), for special displays (*underscore special displays*), or to customers of long standing (*full stop, paragraph*)
(*shoulder heading, initial capitals, underscored*) Pro Forma Invoice
This is // packed with goods sent on approval and is similar to an invoice (*underscore invoice*), except that after goods are chosen from the package and the buyer decides to keep them, an official invoice is then sent as well, and the customer // pays on the invoice (*full stop, paragraph*)
(*shoulder heading, initial capitals, underscored*) Cycle Billing
This is the name given to the system whereby monthly statements are sent out on allotted days in the month, instead of all being sent out at the end of the month (*full stop*) // In a large firm, with a lot of customers, this spreads the work load (*full stop*) Incoming payments are then also spread over the month instead of arriving in a rush altogether within a short time and causing an overload of work // in one period of the month (*full stop, paragraph*)
(*shoulder heading, initial capitals, underscored*) Carriage Paid
The seller pays the carriage (*full stop, paragraph*)

(*shoulder heading, initial capitals, underscored*) Terms
Net Monthly
The full amount shown on the statement of account is due
(*full stop, paragraph*)
(*shoulder heading, initial capitals, underscored*) Cash
Discount
An allowance is offered // to a buyer to induce him to pay
promptly (*full stop*) The rate and period of time allowed are
shown on the monthly statement (*underscore monthly
statement, full stop*)

END OF TASK

The dictation began at point (   ) on the indicator scale.

END OF DICTATION

Unit 5

Notes to the teacher

This unit is going to consist of several A5 letters. A list of the names and addresses to be inserted by the students is given below and should be given to the students in visual form, either in a handout (which is probably easier from the point of view that the students will be at different stages of the course by this time) or on the chalkboard or OHP. Each address should be numbered as shown. The students will be asked to produce the letters on A5 paper, in the fully-blocked style, with open punctuation, using the teacher's initials and their own as a reference. They will use today's date. Some revision may be necessary.

Names and addresses

17 Mr J Greeves
   26 Davenport Road
   LONDON
   SW1 26T

18 Mr E Brown
   19 Lee Street
   ROMFORD
   Essex
   RM9 6GE

19 The Housing Manager
   County Hall
   Country Lane
   SOUTH CROYDON
   Surrey
   CR2 8JJ

20 Mrs A Johnson
   34 The Grove
   HALESOWEN
   Birmingham
   B62 3KR

21 The Manager
   Corrin Travel Agency
   The Broadway
   CROWBOROUGH
   Sussex
   TN6 1AB

22 Miss S Adams
   3 Norfolk Road
   TUNBRIDGE WELLS
   Kent
   TN1 3TD

This is unit 5

In this unit you will be doing the type of work normally carried out by an audio-typist. We will begin with several short letters – all to be typed on A5 paper. Make sure you have a dictionary and use it if in doubt. Remember that even <u>one</u> error of any kind means the letter cannot be signed by the employer and is, therefore, useless. A list of names and addresses will be given to you by your teacher. One name and address is to be inserted in each letter. The addresses are numbered to correspond with the tasks. Type the correct address with the right letter. Use your teacher's initials and your own as a reference on each

letter and use today's date. Use the fully-blocked style of
display and open punctuation.
     For the next task put a sheet of A5 paper into the
machine. Set equal margins. Type in the reference and
date. Using the list of addresses, type in the first one.
You should now be ready for dictation.
Are you ready for the first letter?

This is task 17

Dear Sir
Thank you for your letter of 21 June, enquiring about our new
line in pine kitchen furniture (*full stop*) We hope that the
following information will help you (*full stop, paragraph*)
We manufacture pine furniture such as tables with matching
chairs as well // as kitchen cabinets (*full stop*) In
addition we manufacture matching kitchen utensils such as
table (*hyphen*) mats, pine bowls and trays (*full stop,
paragraph*)
Enclosed is a table showing the prices of our equipment and
the addresses of stores which stock our goods (*full stop,
paragraph*)
If there is any // further information you need, please do
not hesitate to contact us again (*full stop*)
Yours faithfully

                                              END OF TASK

The dictation began at point (   ) on the indicator scale.
Check your work THOROUGHLY.

                                          END OF DICTATION

Follow the same procedure as for the first letter.
  (1) A5 paper;
  (2) set the margins;
  (3) type the reference and date and
  (4) type in the address.

Are you ready?

This is task 18

Dear Sir
We are writing to inform you of the (*initial capitals*)
Annual General Meeting of our sports club, of which you are
a member (*full stop, paragraph*)
The meeting will be held at the sports club hall on Friday 1
July and will be // mainly concerned with the renovation of
the old sports club in (*initial capitals*) Park Crescent
(*full stop, paragraph*)
We hope that you will attend the meeting which begins at
seventeen hundred hours and look forward to seeing you (*full
stop*)
Yours faithfully

                                              END OF TASK

The dictation began at point (   ) on the indicator scale.

END OF DICTATION

You should now know the procedure before typing the body of the letter.
Are you ready?

This is task 19

Dear Sir
I am writing to ask if you could give me some information regarding three (*hyphen*) bedroomed accommodation in the Surrey area (*full stop*) With regard to price (*pound sign*) seventy thousand is the most I could afford to pay (*full stop, paragraph*)
At the moment I am living // in London but wish to move to Surrey as my work will shortly take me there (*full stop, paragraph*)
Your help would be much appreciated (*full stop*)
Yours faithfully

END OF TASK

The dictation began at point (   ) on the indicator scale.

END OF DICTATION

This is task 20

Dear Madam
Thank you for your letter of 20 June enquiring about materials suitable for use as seat covers (*full stop, paragraph*)
We make a wide range of materials and many of these are suitable for use in making seat covers (*full stop*) For example, // we manufacture materials such as light (*hyphen*) weight stretch nylon and for a really luxurious look we make velvet seat covers in a range of colours (*full stop, paragraph*)
We are enclosing a catalogue showing all the kinds of seat covers that we manufacture, along // with their prices (*full stop*) We hope that this is of use to you (*full stop*)
Yours faithfully HOUSEHOLD FABRICS LIMITED Manager

END OF TASK

The dictation began at point (   ) on the indicator scale.

END OF DICTATION

This is task 21
Dear Sir

I feel that I must write to you to complain about the behaviour of one of your employees (*full stop, paragraph*)

On 24 June I came into your travel agency to make a coach reservation for a one (*hyphen*) day trip to Blackpool (*full stop*) // Your assistant, Miss Clapton, was not only very abrupt in her manner but was quite rude to me (*full stop*) I am sure that her attitude will discourage customers from doing business with your agency (*full stop*)

Yours faithfully

END OF TASK

The dictation began at point ( ) on the indicator scale.

END OF DICTATION

This is task 22
Dear Miss Adams

Thank you for returning the application form (*full stop, paragraph*)

We are pleased to say that you have been selected for an interview and we would like you to attend on Monday 28 June at eleven hundred hours (*full stop*) On your arrival // will you report to the receptionist on the ground floor (*question mark, paragraph*)

Please bring with you your birth certificate and any educational certificates (*full stop, paragraph*)

We look forward to seeing you (*full stop*)

Yours sincerely D S BROWN Personnel Manager

END OF TASK

The dictation began at point ( ) on the indicator scale.

END OF DICTATION

28

Unit 6

Notes to the teacher

This unit consists of six short memos. It is preferable that all students should have printed memo forms. A reference will not be included in the instructions to students. If the teacher feels that this is necessary, it may be included. In the second section of the work the students will be asked to make an extra copy. It is suggested that the blocked style of layout is used.

This is unit 6

Each of the following tasks is a short memo. Each one should be typed on a printed A5 memo form. Use the blocked style of layout and insert today's date.
Are you ready for the memos?

This is task 23

To: All members of staff From: The Manager
Subject: Luncheon Vouchers
You will be glad to hear that as from next Friday luncheon vouchers will be issued to all members of staff (*full stop, paragraph*)
The vouchers will total (*pound sign*) two point five oh, each voucher being worth fifty pence and // you will receive five vouchers at the end of the week with your wages (*full stop*)

                                             END OF TASK

The dictation began at point ( ) on the indicator scale.

                                             END OF DICTATION

This is task 24

To: The Secretary From: The Chairman
It has been suggested that a charity show be organised for handicapped children at St. John's Hospital (*full stop*) The show is to be on Saturday 6 August at eleven hundred hours (*full stop, paragraph*)
Will you please notify all members of // the committee (*question mark, paragraph*)
Tickets can be obtained in advance from the club or at the door (*full stop*) The usual light refreshments will be provided (*full stop*)

                                             END OF TASK

The dictation began at point (   ) on the indicator scale.

END OF DICTATION

This is task 25
To: All Drivers   From: The Managing Director
Subject: Parking Fines
Please note that parking fines received while in a firm's
car are to be paid by the drivers (*full stop*) They are not
the responsibility of the firm (*full stop, paragraph*)
Any fines received at (*initial capitals*) Head Office, which //
are unpaid, will be deducted from the driver's salary (*full
stop*)

END OF TASK

The dictation began at point (   ) on the indicator scale.

END OF DICTATION

There will now follow three memos.   Would you please make an
extra copy of each.
Are you ready?

This is task 26
To: All Members of Staff   From: The Managing Director
Subject: Staff Training
This store will be closed all day on Monday 16 October in
order that staff training may take place (*full stop,
paragraph*)
All staff should attend as usual on that day, arriving by oh
nine hundred // hours (*full stop, paragraph*)
Talks will be given and films shown for your benefit (*full
stop*) There will also be a period when you, the staff, may
tell us your views and make any suggestions that you think
might improve the running of the store (*full stop, paragraph*)
I hope that it will prove a rewarding day for us all (*full
stop*)

END OF TASK

The dictation began at point (   ) on the indicator scale.
Did you remember to make an extra copy?

END OF DICTATION

This is task 27
To: The Manager   From: The Secretary
Following the recent advertisements of secretarial posts in
our department, several people have applied (*full stop*) I
have arranged for you to interview four of the more suitable
applicants on Wednesday next between ten hundred and twelve
hundred hours (*full stop, paragraph*)

Their // ages range from seventeen to twenty-two and they all
have the necessary qualifications required for the posts
(*full stop*) Their names are Joan Smith, John Brady, Pat
Brown and Margaret Howard (*full stop*)

END OF TASK

The dictation began at point ( ) on the indicator scale.

END OF DICTATION

This is task 28

To: Members of the Social Club Committee
From: The Chairman   Subject: Redecoration
Please note that as from 2 November, the club will be closed
for redecoration (*full stop, paragraph*)
We hope to have it open again by 14 December, in time for
our fancy dress dance // which is to be held on 18 December,
in aid of the club's tenth anniversary (*full stop, paragraph*)
We are sorry for any trouble and inconvenience that this
may cause, but look forward to seeing you at the dance (*full
stop*)

END OF TASK

The dictation began at point ( ) on the indicator scale.

END OF DICTATION

Unit 7

Notes to the teacher

The following unit contains six A4 letters. The students
will be asked to type an envelope for four of the letters
and make extra copies for two of them. Some of the letters
will contain a subject heading and the fully-blocked style
is suggested. Again, a handout will be needed, showing the
following names and addresses.

Names and addresses

29 The Manager
    Williams & Old Ltd
    Sandy Street
    LEICESTER
    LE2 6JL

30 Mr H Wallen
    26 Hempstead Road
    CROYDON
    Surrey
    CR6 2TP

31 Mr F T Hampshire
    General Manager
    Neon Wholesale Co
    Strand Grove
    LONDON
    SW1E 6HD

32 Mrs S Thompson
    113 Roycraft Avenue
    MANSFIELD
    Nottingham
    NG5 2RJ

33 Mrs D Burke
    3 Fanshawe Crescent
    BARROW-IN-FURNESS
    Cumbria
    CU3 6TR

34 Mrs C T Davies
    38 Burnham Court
    ABERDEEN
    AB2 6SB

This is unit 7

You will now produce several A4 letters. Some of the spelling may be a little difficult so make sure you have your
dictionary. Use A4 paper and a suitable margin on either
side. Use open punctuation, the fully-blocked style of
layout, insert today's date and your teacher's initials and
your own as a reference. The names and addresses will be
given to you.
Are you ready for the letters?

This is task 29
Dear Sir
We are in urgent need of the materials ordered from you
nearly three months ago (*full stop, paragraph*)
In your quotation for these materials you promised that
delivery would be completed within one month of receipt of

an order and it // was on that basis that we placed the
order with you (*full stop*, *paragraph*)
It is now nearly three months since we placed that order
with you and you have not yet started delivery (*full stop*)
We must ask you to do so immediately and // to complete
delivery of the whole order within the next seven days (*full
stop*, *paragraph*)
We trust that our needs will be met and shall be glad to
have your assurance of this, by telephone, as soon as you
receive this letter (*full stop*)
Yours // faithfully

END OF TASK

The dictation began at point ( ) on the indicator scale.

END OF DICTATION

This is task 30
Dear Sir
Thank you for your letter of 6 February (*full stop*) We have
given very careful consideration to the possibility of
manufacturing the machine you have designed (*full stop*,
paragraph)
We are very impressed and think that it could go some way to
solving // our production problems (*full stop*)
Unfortunately, at this stage we are not in a position to buy
the total rights to the machine, but we are prepared to
consider your alternative suggestion that we should
partially finance the project (*full stop*, *paragraph*)
If this arrangement // would still be of interest to you,
would you please telephone our office and arrange for an
appointment with me (*full stop*)
Yours faithfully, Manager

END OF TASK

The dictation began at point ( ) on the indicator scale.

END OF DICTATION

Some letters may contain a subject heading which comes after
the salutation and before the first paragraph. If you are
only told "heading" with no specific instructions, type the
heading as you have been instructed by your teacher.
    Type an envelope for this letter.

Are you ready?

This is task 31
Dear Sir
(*heading*) MISS JOAN TUCKER Thank you for your letter of 6
December (*full stop*) I will certainly answer your queries
about Miss Tucker (*full stop*, *paragraph*)

She was appointed as a shorthand (*hyphen*) typist five years ago after completing a one (*hyphen*) year, full (*hyphen*) time secretarial course at a // technical college (*full stop*) Her qualifications were excellent and we were more than happy to appoint her (*full stop, paragraph*)
During the five years she has been with us, she has been promoted three times and for the last two years she has been my (*initial capitals*) Personal // Secretary (*full stop*) This is a very responsible job and Miss Tucker copes admirably (*full stop, paragraph*)
She is quiet, efficient, pleasant in manner and very popular with her colleagues (*full stop*) I cannot speak too highly of her (*full stop*)
Yours faithfully Managing Director

END OF TASK

The dictation began at point ( ) on the indicator scale.

END OF DICTATION

Type an envelope for this letter

This is task 32

Dear Madam
Please accept my apologies for the delay in replying to your letter of 24 May (*full stop*) With reference to your enquiry, you will appreciate that any offer of accommodation is subject to availability and the offer made was the best we could tender at the time (*full stop, paragraph*)
I feel that there must have been some misunderstanding regarding three (*hyphen*) bedroomed accommodation as any reference made to a three (*hyphen*) bedroomed house was made prior to the birth of your second son, when there was still the // possibility of opposite sexes necessitating a three (*hyphen*) bedroomed unit (*full stop, paragraph*)
It is now our policy that families with two children of the same sex are allocated two (*hyphen*) bedroomed houses (*full stop, paragraph*)
I note that you now will consider a two (*hyphen*) bedroomed house and we will endeavour // to make you a further offer of accommodation as soon as possible, but this can only be done when a suitable vacancy occurs (*full stop*)
Yours faithfully Housing Manager

END OF TASK

The dictation began at point ( ) on the indicator scale.
Have you remembered the envelope?

END OF DICTATION

Are you ready?

34

This is task 33
Dear Madam
(*heading*) TRANSFER OF ACCOMMODATION With reference to your
letter of 4 November I must advise you that in order to be
fair to all (*underscore all*) applicants, houses are allocated to the tenants of flats according to the length of //
continuous council tenancy in such accommodation (*full stop*)
Applications for houses are not registered until the applicant has at least a four (*hyphen*) year tenancy (*full stop*,
paragraph)
Accordingly, I am unable to consider your request for transfer to a house at this time, and, bearing in // mind your
short period of tenancy at your present address, it is
likely to be some time before your request will be
considered (*full stop*, *paragraph*)
Following your request for a more modern low (*hyphen*) rise flat
the (*initial capitals*) Estate Management Officer did endeavour
to // visit you in October to discuss the matter, but despite
numerous visits he was unable to make contact (*full stop*)
Yours faithfully Housing Manager

END OF TASK

The dictation began at point (   ) on the indicator scale.

END OF DICTATION

Make an extra copy of this letter and type an envelope.
Are you ready?

This is task 34
Dear Mrs Davies
(*heading*) EXAMINATION ENTRANCE FEES   I regret to inform you
that the (*initial capitals*) Examinations Committee, at a
recent meeting, agreed that as from 1 January next all fees
will be increased (*full stop*, *paragraph*)
The examination entrance fee for the (*initial capitals*)
Council's higher grade // examinations will be increased to
(*pound sign*) eight per paper (*full stop*) If a candidate is
absent because of illness or accident and a doctor's certificate is produced, the fee, less (*pound sign*) one, will be
refunded (*full stop*) The fee for all other grades of examinations
will // now be (*pound sign*) six point five oh (*full stop*,
paragraph)
A charge of (*pound sign*) four will be made to any candidate
wishing to enter for the examination after the official closing
date (*full stop*, *paragraph*)
Full details of these increases will be included in our new
booklet which will be issued // next month (*full stop*)
Yours sincerely S WILLIAMS Examinations Secretary

END OF TASK

35

The dictation began at point (   ) on the indicator scale.

END OF DICTATION

Unit 8

Notes to the teacher

This unit is not "counted" as dictation. Students will be asked to estimate paper size and to type an inside address from dictation. There is also a list, a letter requiring several copies and a report about a word processing software package.

This is unit 8

Read the passage in the "Reference" section concerning "Estimating Paper Sizes". You are now going to type a letter of about 80 words. Use headed paper and make a second copy. Instructions are included.
Are you ready?

This is task 35

Our reference is M (*for Mary*), D (*for David*) (*oblique*) K S (*for Samuel*). Use today's date. The letter is addressed to Mr Paul Williams, 21 Hill View Drive, Edinburgh EH14 6P (*for Peter*), B (*for Benjamin*). The letter reads:
Dear Mr Williams
(*heading, capitals*) INCREASES IN FARES As you are a regular customer of this agency, we are enclosing our latest schedule showing the new increases in fares (*full stop*)
These take effect from 30 May (*full stop, paragraph*)
We must point out that flights booked for overseas countries will be affected, even if the booking is made before 30 May (*full stop, paragraph*)
We hope we will have the pleasure of handling your arrangements again (*full stop*)
Yours sincerely
(*Addition: after the words "INCREASES IN" in the heading, add the word "AIR"*)

END OF TASK

The dictation began at point ( ) on the indicator scale.

END OF DICTATION

You are now going to produce a short list with a main heading. Use suitable display. Note that any special instructions will be preceded by the word "typist".
Are you ready?

This is task 36
(*heading, capitals, underscored*) <u>BANK SERVICES</u> The following list shows some of the services offered by banks (*full stop; typist: there now follows a display of five numbered paragraphs*) (1) Deposit accounts (*dash*) to save money (*full stop*) (2) Current accounts (*full stop*) (3) Loans to customers (*full stop*) (4) Night banking (*full stop*) (5) Ways of paying bills (*colon; typist: there now follows a display of four sub-headings*) (a) Cheque cards (*full stop*) (b) Standing orders (*full stop*) (c) Credit cards (*full stop*) (d) Bank (*initial capital*) Giro credit (*full stop*)

END OF TASK

The dictation began at point ( ) on the indicator scale. Check your work for accuracy as well as display.

END OF DICTATION

In the "model answers" section you will find a handwritten letter (Task 37 Part A on page 66). Read that letter, then type a reply using the notes which will be dictated. Follow the procedure given in the "Reference" section. Read these instructions carefully.
   It will take some time before you can do this quickly. Practice makes perfect!
   Here are the notes for reply to the letter on page 66.

This is task 37
Apologize for delay. The assistant who took the order has left. Order placed on day Mr Bramley telephoned. Can he wait one more week? Money refunded if this is not satisfactory.

END OF TASK

The dictation began at point ( ) on the indicator scale.

END OF DICTATION

There now follows a short letter to a doctor. Please type an envelope and produce three copies of the letter.

This is task 38
To Dr E Fredricks (F-R-E-D-R-I-C-K-S), 27 The Crescent, Manchester, M(*for Mary*) S13 3TE. (*Typist: Please mark the letter confidential*)
Dear Dr Fredricks
Thank you for your letter of last week regarding your patient, Mrs Jane (J-A-N-E) Andrews (*full stop, paragraph*) As a result of that letter we carried out further tests and the papers are enclosed (*full stop*) Mrs Andrews is, as yet, unaware of the results but was told by the hospital to

contact you within 14 (figures) days of the tests (*full stop*)
Perhaps you would be kind enough to tell her the results,
which should put her mind at rest (*full stop, paragraph*)
If she is still concerned, do ask her to contact me again (*full
stop*) Yours sincerely   G STEVENS (S-T-E-V-E-N-S) Chief
Consultant

END OF TASK

The dictation began at point (   ) on the indicator scale.

END OF DICTATION

The next piece of work is a report on the advantages of a
particular word processing software package.   It has four
paragraphs, three of them requiring shoulder headings.
Are you ready?

This is task 39

(*heading, capitals, underscored*) Advantages of the   (*open
quotes*) Microtwo (M-I-C-R-O-T-W-O) Software Package (*close
quotes*)
Microtwo is easy to install on your system (*full stop*) All
that is required is to follow the step (*hyphen*) by
(*hyphen*) step instructions and the software is loaded (*full
stop*) It allows you to take advantage of all the memory that
comes with the machine, and any additional memory can be
added later (*full stop, paragraph*) (*Typist: type the next
three paragraphs with shoulder headings*)
(*heading, capitals*) SPREADSHEETS Microtwo uses memory
only for cells (C-E-L-L-S) that contain data, allowing for
more efficient memory use (*full stop*) Calculations can be
done manually or automatically and only the cells affected
by a change are calculated, rather than the whole
spreadsheet (*full stop, paragraph*)
(*heading, capitals*) BUSINESS GRAPHICS   There are (*figures*) 40
predesigned charts in this package in (*figures*) 7 basic
types: (*colon*) area, bar, column, line, pie, scatter (S-C-A-
T-T-E-R) and combinations (*full stop, paragraph*)
(*heading, capitals*) DATABASE Microtwo's integrated database
makes it easy to organise, file, sort and retrieve any data
according to your needs (*full stop*) You can sort through
thousands of records in seconds.

END OF TASK

The dictation began at point (   ) on the indicator scale.

END OF DICTATION

39

MODEL ANSWERS

Task 1

Thank you for your letter.

I hope you will come.

They say it is easy.

We agree with them.

The prices are very low.

Would you agree with that?

We shall see you tomorrow.

They seem to have problems.

Is that very common?

I think it is common.

Task 2

Thank you for your letter of yesterday.

I hope you will come to the factory.

They say it is easy to find.

We agree with them that it is.

We feel the prices are very low.

Would you agree that they are?

We shall see you tomorrow if you wish.

They seem to have problems just now.

Do you think that it is common?

I do think it is quite common.

Task 3

I am happy to enclose a bank statement.

The meeting I have attended was successful.

We were able to transfer a large sum of money.

When shall I receive your cheque in payment?

The bank is expecting to receive a cheque.

The inspector was completely satisfied with the report.

I hope you were successful in your recent test.

We shall be happy to come to the meeting tomorrow.

Do you have a bank account?

I hope you found the talk useful.

Task 4

I am happy to enclose a bank statement giving full details.

The meeting I have attended was successful and useful.

We were able to transfer a large sum of money to your account.

When shall I receive your cheque in payment of the goods?

The bank is expecting to receive a cheque from you soon.

The inspector was completely satisfied with the report given to him.

I hope the recent tests proved to be successful.

We shall be happy to meet you for a talk tomorrow.

Do you have a cheque book and a statement?

I hope you found the talk completely to your satisfaction.

Task 5

Many thanks for your letter of yesterday.

I was hoping we could go to the coast.

If the weather remains good we shall go.

We have several friends who live there.

Shall we drive there or go on the train?

Perhaps we can stay with our friends.

If not we can stay at a local hotel.

The rates they charge are very reasonable.

Task 6 Part A

The new forms - the green ones - are now being used.

Our directors - there are three - have given their permission.

Do come to see us - you are always welcome.

Last week - on Wednesday - he resigned.

Task 6 Part B

We are the greatest!

Go abroad this year!

Hurry up or we shall be late!

Task 6 Part C

You will be allowed three days (the maximum) for travel.

The girl (the young one) came home.

Task 7

It is hoped to be able to accommodate you.

The hotel manager was certain he had vacant accommodation.

Our neighbour was very good to us.

The meeting is extremely important to them.

They asked if you were all right.

Do you know the height of the building?

You will need to be familiar with these words.

The results of the tests (the latest) were excellent.

The doctor said he was completely recovered.

Task 8

The manager feels that, by Friday, a decision must be made.

If you are to obtain a job, you should be bright, cheerful and dedicated.

You cannot expect to get a cheque, cash and a gift.

I hope the boy, John, will be happy in his work.

The accommodation was reasonably priced, very comfortable and warm.

The audience was extremely happy and cheered loudly.

Task 9

I am going on Monday: Jim is coming too.

Mr Shephard lives in Leicester.

It rained yesterday; it rained again this morning.

The switch was on/off.

Money owed to someone else is called a liability.

One is white; the other is black.

These are valuable stones: emerald, diamond and sapphire.

Task 10

When you leave school and start work, you will probably need
a bank account. There are two main types of account —
current and deposit. A current account is one into which
cheques are paid. You are given a cheque book.

If you found that you could afford to save some money, you
could open a deposit account. You are paid interest on the
money you put into a deposit account. (It is a useful way
of saving money.)

Banks provide many services for their customers. If you
decide to go abroad for your holiday, the bank will provide
you with currency. They can also help with insurance, loans
and many other things.

Task 11

Why do people diet? People diet because they think they are
too plump or because they are overweight. The extent to
which you diet is very important — it could be dangerous —
be careful! If you are very overweight, a visit to your
doctor might be helpful.

Do you ever look back at your past? If you do, have you
realised just how much you have changed? Your hair may be
longer or shorter and you may have gained or lost weight.
Your whole pattern of life may have altered considerably.
The things you used to enjoy doing, now hold no pleasure for
you and your tastes in food and music may have changed
greatly.

Is owning a car an advantage or a disadvantage? It has one
important advantage and that is that it enables you to
travel without having to rely on public transport or your
feet. Although it is expensive nowadays to run a car, it is
pleasant to travel in the comfort of your own transport.
Perhaps the biggest disadvantage is the number of accidents
occurring on the roads.

Task 12

When you obtain a job as a secretary, it is quite likely that you will be asked to take the minutes of a meeting. These provide a very necessary record of the important points discussed at the meeting. You will take down, in note form, details of the decisions reached and also the exact wording of every resolution passed. Nothing of importance must be omitted.

The committee's decisions must be recorded in the minutes and the secretary must ensure that she notes all the arguments for and against major decisions. Occasionally a mistake may be found in the minutes and this should be corrected before the minutes are signed. Once they have been signed, they should not be altered in any way.

When typing the minutes, they must be recorded in the correct order. It is usual to begin with details such as time and date of meeting, followed by names of those people present with the chairman's name first on the list. Then the minutes of the last meeting are read and any matters arising from the minutes are discussed. After this, the general business is dealt with and this is followed by an item called "any other business".

Task 13

Thank you for your letter of 21 June, enquiring about our new line in pine kitchen furniture. We hope that the following information will help you.

We manufacture pine furniture such as tables with matching chairs as well as kitchen cabinets. In addition we manufacture matching kitchen utensils such as table-mats, fruit-salad bowls and trays.

Enclosed is a table showing the prices of our equipment and the addresses of stores which stock our goods.

If there is any further information you need, please do not hesitate to contact us again.

Task 14

The best time for the tourist to visit Holland is during these three months: June, July and August. It is mild and there is plenty of sunshine. The weather's often good in September, but anyone going outside the summer season should choose the Spring months (April and May), when the bulb fields are in flower.

There are a number of ways of getting to Holland. It is possible to go from London by rail or by road – both routes require the use of a ferry. There are direct air services from London to Amsterdam and Rotterdam, and from Manchester to Amsterdam.

The famous Dutch "clogs" are on sale everywhere and are still in everyday use. Women in national dress can be seen in the villages, especially on Sundays. It is impossible to be in Holland for more than a brief spell without noticing how fond of music and singing the Dutch are. As likely as not, the quiet of an evening stroll in a small town will be interrupted by the strains of the local band at practice.

Task 15 part A

The Managing Director asked everyone to be in the Board Room in good time for the meeting. He wished to discuss some proposed major changes in the firm's policy. The Annual General Meeting was to take place on Friday next and a decision would need to be taken before then.

Task 15 part B

At present the subscription to the Sports Club is £8.25. It was proposed that this should be increased to £10.75 per year. The increase of £2.50 would help to cover the costs of better facilities.

Task 15 part C

The meeting was due to begin at 1400 hours but it had to be delayed in order that the Chairman had time to travel from Cardiff to attend the meeting. At 1630 hours the meeting began and did not finish until 1800 hours.

The girl had to attend the offices of Smith & Freeman Limited for an interview at 0900 hours. Owing to a bus strike, however, she was unable to go for the interview. She did not know what to do so she did nothing - except go back home. What should she have done? She should have telephoned the firm to offer an explanation - she could have asked for another appointment.

Task 16

TERMS USED IN SELLING

Monthly Credit

Goods are paid for at the end of the month. Often a cash discount is then allowed.

Trade Discount

An allowance, usually called a percentage, is given to enable
the wholesaler or retailer to make a profit. It is also given
to encourage bulk buying, for special displays, or to customers
of long standing.

Pro Forma Invoice

This is packed with goods sent on approval and is similar to
an invoice, except that after goods are chosen from the package
and the buyer decides to keep them, an official invoice is then
sent as well, and the customer pays on the invoice.

Cycle Billing

This is the name given to the system whereby monthly statements
are sent out on allotted days in the month, instead of all
being sent out at the end of the month. In a large firm, with
a lot of customers, this spreads the work load. Incoming
payments are then also spread over the month instead of
arriving in a rush altogether within a short time and causing
an overload of work in one period of the month.

Carriage Paid

The seller pays the carriage.

Terms Net Monthly

The full amount shown on the statement of account is due.

Cash Discount

An allowance is offered to a buyer to induce him to pay
promptly. The rate and period of time allowed are shown on
the monthly statement.

Task 17

(Reference)

(Date)

Mr J Greeves
26 Davenport Road
LONDON
SW1 26T

Dear Sir

Thank you for your letter of 21 June enquiring about our new
line in pine kitchen furniture. We hope that the following
information will help you.

We manufacture pine furniture such as tables with matching
chairs as well as kitchen cabinets. In addition we manufacture matching kitchen utensils such as table-mats, pine
bowls and trays.

Enclosed is a table showing the prices of our equipment and
the addresses of stores which stock our goods.

If there is any further information you need, please do not
hesitate to contact us again.

Yours faithfully

Enc

Task 18

(Reference)

(Date)

Mr E Brown
19 Lee Street
ROMFORD
Essex
RM9 6GE

Dear Sir

We are writing to inform you of the Annual
General Meeting of our sports club, of which
you are a member.

The meeting will be held at the sports club
hall on Friday 1 July and will be mainly concerned with the renovation of the old sports
club in Park Crescent.

We hope that you will attend the meeting which
begins at 1700 hours and look forward to seeing
you.

Yours faithfully

Task 19

(Date)

The Housing Manager
County Hall
Country Lane
SOUTH CROYDON
Surrey
CR2 8JJ

Dear Sir

I am writing to ask if you could give me some
information regarding three-bedroomed accommodation in the Surrey area. With regard to
price, £70,000 is the most I could afford to pay.

At the moment I am living in London but wish to
move to Surrey as my work will shortly take me
there.

Your help would be much appreciated.

Yours faithfully

Task 20

(Reference)

(Date)

Mrs A Johnson
34 The Grove
HALESOWEN
Birmingham
B62 3KR

Dear Madam

Thank you for your letter of 20 June enquiring
about materials suitable for use as seat covers.

We make a wide range of materials and many of
these are suitable for use in making seat
covers. For example, we manufacture materials
such as light-weight stretch nylon and for a
really luxurious look we make velvet seat
covers in a range of colours.

We are enclosing a catalogue showing all the
kinds of seat covers that we manufacture,
along with their prices. We hope that this is
of use to you.

Yours faithfully
HOUSEHOLD FABRICS LIMITED

Manager

Enc

Task 21

(Date)

The Manager
Corrin Travel Agency
The Broadway
CROWBOROUGH
Sussex
TN6 1AB

Dear Sir

I feel that I must write to you to complain
about the behaviour of one of your employees.

On 24 June I came into your travel agency to
make a coach reservation for a one-day trip to
Blackpool. Your assistant, Miss Clapton, was
not only very abrupt in her manner but was quite
rude to me. I am sure that her attitude will
discourage customers from doing business with
your agency.

Yours faithfully

Task 22

(Reference)

(Date)

Miss S Adams
3 Norfolk Road
TUNBRIDGE WELLS
Kent
TN1 3TD

Dear Miss Adams

Thank you for returning the application form.

We are pleased to say that you have been
selected for an interview and we would like you
to attend on Monday 28 June at 1100 hours. On
your arrival will you report to the receptionist
on the ground floor?

Please bring with you your birth certificate and
any educational certificates.

We look forward to seeing you.

Yours sincerely

D S BROWN
Personnel Manager

Task 23

To: All Members of Staff

From: The Manager

Luncheon Vouchers

You will be glad to hear that as from next Friday luncheon
vouchers will be issued to all members of staff.

The vouchers will total £2.50, each voucher being worth 50p
and you will receive five vouchers at the end of the week
with your wages.

(Date)

Task 24

To: The Secretary

From: The Chairman

It has been suggested that a charity show be organised for
handicapped children at St. John's Hospital. The show is to be
on Saturday 6 August at 1100 hours.

Will you please notify all members of the committee?

Tickets can be obtained in advance from the club or at the door.
The usual light refreshments will be provided.

(Date)

Task 25

To: All Drivers

From: The Managing Director

Parking Fines

Please note that parking fines received while in a firm's car
are to be paid by the drivers. They are not the responsibility
of the firm.

Any fines received at Head Office, which are unpaid, will be
deducted from the driver's salary.

(Date)

Task 26

To: All Members of Staff

From: The Managing Director

Staff Training

This store will be closed all day on Monday 16 October in order
that staff training may take place.

All staff should attend as usual on that day, arriving by 0900
hours.

Talks will be given and films shown for your benefit. There
will also be a period when you, the staff, may tell us your
views and make any suggestions that you think might improve
the running of the store.

I hope that it will prove a rewarding day for us all.

(Date)

Task 27

To: The Manager

From: The Secretary

Following the recent advertisements of secretarial posts in our
department, several people have applied. I have arranged for
you to interview four of the more suitable applicants on
Wednesday next between 1000 and 1200 hours.

Their ages range from 17 to 22 and they all have the necessary
qualifications required for the posts. Their names are Joan
Smith, John Brady, Pat Brown and Margaret Howard.

(Date)

Task 28

To: Members of the Social Club Committee

From: The Chairman

Redecoration

Please note that as from 2 November, the club will be closed for
redecoration.

We hope to have it open again by 14 December, in time for our
fancy dress dance which is to be held on 18 December, in aid
of the club's tenth anniversary.

We are sorry for any trouble and inconvenience that this may
cause, but look forward to seeing you at the dance.

(Date)

Task 29

(Reference)

(Date)

The Manager
Williams & Old Ltd
Sandy Street
LEICESTER
LE2 6JL

Dear Sir

We are in urgent need of the materials ordered from you nearly
three months ago.

In your quotation for these materials you promised that
delivery would be completed within one month of receipt of an
order and it was on that basis that we placed the order with
you.

It is now nearly three months since we placed that order with
you and you have not yet started delivery. We must ask you to
do so immediately and to complete delivery of the whole order
within the next seven days.

We trust that our needs will be met and shall be glad to have
your assurance of this, by telephone, as soon as you receive
this letter.

Yours faithfully

Task 30

(Reference)

(Date)

Mr H Wallen
26 Hempstead Road
CROYDON
Surrey
CR6 2TP

Dear Sir

Thank you for your letter of 6 February. We have given very careful consideration to the possibility of manufacturing the machine you have designed.

We are very impressed and think that it could go some way to solving our production problems. Unfortunately, at this stage we are not in a position to buy the total rights to the machine, but we are prepared to consider your alternative suggestion that we should partially finance the project.

If this arrangement would still be of interest to you, would you please telephone our office and arrange for an appointment with me.

Yours faithfully

Manager

Task 31

(Reference)

(Date)

Mr F T Hampshire
General Manager
Neon Wholesale Co
Strand Grove
LONDON
SW1E 6HD

Dear Sir

MISS JOAN TUCKER

Thank you for your letter of 6 December. I will certainly answer your queries about Miss Tucker.

She was appointed as a shorthand-typist five years ago after completing a one-year, full-time secretarial course at a technical college. Her qualifications were excellent and we were more than happy to appoint her.

During the five years she has been with us, she has been promoted three times and for the last two years she has been my Personal Secretary. This is a very responsible job and Miss Tucker copes admirably.

She is quiet, efficient, pleasant in manner and very popular with her colleagues. I cannot speak too highly of her.

Yours faithfully

```
Mr F T Hampshire
General Manager
Neon Wholesale Co
Strand Grove
LONDON
SW1E 6HD
```

Managing Director

Task 32

(Reference)

(Date)

Mrs S Thompson
113 Roycraft Avenue
MANSFIELD
Nottingham
NG5 2RJ

Dear Madam

Please accept my apologies for the delay in replying to your
letter of 24 May. With reference to your enquiry, you will
appreciate that any offer of accommodation is subject to
availability and the offer made was the best we could tender
at the time.

I feel that there must have been some misunderstanding regarding
three-bedroomed accommodation as any reference made to a three-
bedroomed house was made prior to the birth of your second son,
when there was still the possibility of opposite sexes necessitating a three-bedroomed unit.

It is now our policy that families with two children of the
same sex are allocated two-bedroomed houses.

I note that you now will consider a two-bedroomed house and we
will endeavour to make you a further offer of accommodation as
soon as possible, but this can only be done when a suitable
vacancy occurs.

Yours faithfully

> Mrs S Thompson
> 113 Roycraft Avenue
> MANSFIELD
> Nottingham
> NG5 2RJ

Housing Manager

Task 33

(Reference)

(Date)

Mrs D Burke
3 Fanshawe Crescent
BARROW-IN-FURNESS
Cumbria
CU3 6TR

Dear Madam

TRANSFER OF ACCOMMODATION

With reference to your letter of 4 November I must advise you
that in order to be fair to all applicants, houses are allocated
to the tenants of flats according to the length of continuous
council tenancy in such accommodation. Applications for houses
are not registered until the applicant has at least a four-year
tenancy.

Accordingly, I am unable to consider your request for transfer
to a house at this time, and, bearing in mind your short period
of tenancy at your present address, it is likely to be some time
before your request will be considered.

Following your request for a more modern low-rise flat the
Estate Management Officer did endeavour to visit you in October
to discuss the matter, but despite numerous visits he was
unable to make contact.

Yours faithfully

Housing Manager

Mrs D Burke
3 Fanshawe Crescent
BARROW-IN-FURNESS
Cumbria
CU3 6TR

62

Task 34

(Reference)

(Date)

Mrs C T Davies
38 Burnham Court
ABERDEEN
AB2 6SB

Dear Mrs Davies

EXAMINATION ENTRANCE FEES

I regret to inform you that the Examinations Committee, at a recent meeting, agreed that as from 1 January next all fees will be increased.

The examination entrance fee for the Council's higher grade examinations will be increased to £8 per paper. If a candidate is absent because of illness or accident and a doctor's certificate is produced, the fee, less £1, will be refunded. The fee for all other grades of examinations will now be £6.50.

A charge of £4 will be made to any candidate wishing to enter for the examination after the official closing date.

Full details of these increases will be included in our new booklet which will be issued next month.

Yours sincerely

```
Mrs C T Davies
38 Burnham Court
ABERDEEN
AB2 6SB
```

S WILLIAMS
Examinations Secretary

Task 35

Ref MD/KS

(Date)

Mr Paul Williams
21 Hill View Drive
EDINBURGH
EH14 6PB

Dear Mr Williams

INCREASES IN AIR FARES

As you are a regular customer of this agency, we are
enclosing our latest schedule showing the new increases
in fares. These take effect from 30 May.

We must point out that flights booked for overseas countries
will be affected, even if the booking is made before 30 May.

We hope we will have the pleasure of handling your arrangements again.

Yours sincerely

Enc

TASK 36

<u>BANK SERVICES</u>

The following list shows some of the
services offered by banks.

1. Deposit accounts - to save money.

2. Current accounts.

3. Loans to customers.

4. Night banking.

5. Ways of paying bills:

    (a) Cheque cards.
    (b) Standing orders.
    (c) Credit cards.
    (d) Bank Giro credit.

169 Third Avenue
New Cross
London
SE5 36B

The XYZ Record Shop
36 Bishop Street
London
SC2B 6JP

Dear Sir/Madam

On the 16th I ordered the record called
"GREATEST HITS". I was told that it would
be available in approximately one week, and the
assistant (a tall blonde) told me that
she would notify me as soon as it was
available. That was 6 weeks ago.

Today I telephoned and no trace could
be found of either the record or the
order.

I paid £8.75. Please send the record
within 3 days or refund my money.

Yours faithfully

J BRAMLEY

Task 38

(Date)

Dr E Fredricks
27 The Crescent
MANCHESTER
MS13 3TE

CONFIDENTIAL

Dear Dr Fredricks

Thank you for your letter of last week regarding your
patient, Mrs Jane Andrews.

As a result of that letter we carried out further tests
and the papers are enclosed. Mrs Andrews is, as yet,
unaware of the results but was told by the hospital to
contact you within 14 days of the tests. Perhaps you
would be kind enough to tell her the results, which should
put her mind at rest.

If she is still concerned, do ask her to contact me again.

Yours sincerely

> Confidential
>
> Dr E Fredricks
> 27 The Crescent
> MANCHESTER
> MS13 3TE

G STEVENS
Chief Consultant

Enc

Task 39

ADVANTAGES OF THE "MICROTWO SOFTWARE PACKAGE"

Microtwo is easy to install on your system. All that is required is
to follow the step-by-step instructions and the software is loaded.
It allows you to take advantage of all the memory that comes with the
machine, and any additional memory can be added later.

SPREADSHEETS

Microtwo uses memory only for cells that contain data, allowing for
more efficient memory use. Calculations can be done manually or
automatically and only the cells affected by a change are calculated,
rather than the whole spreadsheet.

BUSINESS GRAPHICS

There are 40 predesigned charts in this package in 7 basic types:
area, bar, column, line, pie, scatter and combinations.

DATABASE

Microtwo's integrated database makes it easy to organise, file, sort
and retrieve any data according to your needs. You can sort through
thousands of records in seconds.

REFERENCE SECTION

Estimating paper sizes – indexing

In audio-typing examinations and at work, you may not be told which size of paper to use, and may have to make the decision yourself.

For examination purposes you will often be told how many words each passage contains and from that you can judge the size of paper to use. Here is a guide:

Elite type

Letter of under 120 words (without heading)	– A5
Letter of over 120 words	– A4
Memo of under 150 words	– A5
Memo of over 150 words	– A4

Pica type

Letter of under 100 words (without heading)	– A5
Letter of over 100 words	– A4
Memo of under 120 words	– A5
Memo of over 120 words	– A4

At work, an employer will often use what is called "indexing". The person dictating can mark the beginning of each passage on the index, showing roughly how long each dictated passage lasts. The index is divided into sections, usually covering the number of minutes that can be dictated on the cassette. The index may be a piece of paper, or more likely nowadays, it will be a magnetic strip fixed on to the cassette itself. When a piece of dictation is completed, the dictator presses a button on the microphone which puts a mark on the magnetic strip showing where the passage ended and thus showing how many minutes the dictation lasted.

The picture below shows a cassette with magnetic strip. It shows that pieces were dictated and where each passage finished.

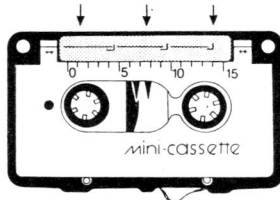

Remember, however, that index slips show only the number of minutes the passage took to be dictated, not the speed of dictation, so you will not know how many words each passage contains. Because indexing can be unreliable, some firms do not use it but may say "this is a long letter", or "this is a short memo", in order to help you to choose the correct size of paper.

The use of the comma

In audio-typing, commas will *not* be dictated to you, so you must think about when to use them. It is usually only necessary to insert the most essential ones.

I will explain the most important uses and give two examples of each.

Commas are used to separate lists of items but are not placed before the word "and".
EXAMPLES:
The girl went shopping to buy cheese, butter, eggs and tomatoes.
Red, yellow, green and blue.

Commas are used to separate words or phrases used as an explanation.
EXAMPLES:
Miss Jones, a fine person, was given the job.
The manager, Mr Thomas, was asked to give a lecture.
Notice that the name (Mr Thomas) explains who the manager is.

Commas are used to separate a number of words that are used to describe something.
EXAMPLES:
The girl was quiet, efficient, pleasant and an asset to the firm.
She was an attractive, tall girl.

The use of the apostrophe

The apostrophe is not dictated and, therefore, you need to
know when to use it.
    These are the most important rules to remember.

   *(1) THE APOSTROPHE SHOWS THAT SOMETHING BELONGS TO
      SOMEONE OR SOMETHING*
      "The boy's toys" means the toys belonging to <u>one</u> boy.
      You need to insert the apostrophe before the <u>"s"</u> of
      boys. This means that the toys belong to the boy.
      If you wanted to say that the toys belonged to several
      boys, then an apostrophe should be inserted after the
      "s" of boys ("The boys' toys".)
      EXAMPLES
      "The girl's coat" means the coat belonging to the
      girl.
      "The man's hat" means the hat belonging to the man.
      "The company's office" means the office belonging to
      one company.
      "The companies' offices" means the offices belonging
      to at least two companies.
      You must work out whether the person dictating means
      a singular word, e.g. "the boy's toys" meaning one
      boy, or a plural, "the boys' toys" meaning several
      boys. You may need to listen a little ahead of what
      you are typing to work this out.

   (2) ITS AND IT'S
      The words "its" and "it's" are often confused.
      "It's" is a shortened version of "it is" and is
      rarely used in business.
      "Its" shows that something belongs to something or
      someone else and so in this case the apostrophe is
      <u>not</u> used.
      EXAMPLE:
      "The cat ate its food" meaning the cat ate the food
      given to it.
      If in doubt, listen to the meaning. If it should be
      "it is", insert an apostrophe to make it "it's".
      EXAMPLE:
      "It's a fine day."

Headings and underscore

When typing main and side headings, instructions will
usually say whether the heading is to be:
    (a) centred or blocked;
    (b) closed or spaced capitals; or lower case with initial
        capitals;
    (c) underscored or not
The instructions will come before the heading.
EXAMPLE:
(*centred heading, closed capitals, underscored*)
terms used in selling.
TERMS USED IN SELLING

When using the blocked style of layout, a main heading can
be typed at the left-hand margin.   Side headings are typed at
the left-hand margin.
EXAMPLE:
(*Shoulder heading, initial capitals, underscored*)
Monthly Credit

Goods are paid for at the end of the month.   Often a cash
discount is then allowed.

Trade Discount

An allowance, usually called a percentage, is given to
enable to wholesaler or retailer to make a profit.

UNDERSCORE
If the words to be underscored are not a heading, the
instruction will come after the words.
EXAMPLE:
He read the newspaper (*underscore newspaper*)
He read the newspaper

Replying to a letter

(1)   Read the letter you are to answer, several times, making
       sure you understand it.
(2)   Type the dictated "notes for reply" on a rough sheet of
       paper.
(3)   Draft your reply in double-line spacing.
(4)   Type the letter, using both the draft and the original
       letter as aids.
(5)   Be careful that you use the correct address.
       (a) You are the person to whom the original letter is
           addressed, e.g. in Task 37(a) you would be working
           for the XYZ Record Shop.
       (b) The sender has placed his address at the top of his or her
           letter, e.g. in Task 37(a) it is 169 Third Avenue,
           New Cross.
       Note: The addresses on your final letter should not be in
       the same places as on the original letter. They should be
       the opposite way around!

Word drills

Task

1	common, problems
2	factory, yesterday, tomorrow
3	receive, completely, enclose, successful, account, attend, transfer, statement, useful, recent cheque/check
4	inspector, expecting
5	weather, remains, several, friends, perhaps, reasonable
6	permission, resigned, welcome, abroad, Wednesday allowed/aloud
7	accommodate, accommodation, all right, certain, excellent, extremely, familiar, vacant, height, important
8	decision, dedicated, expect, comfortable, audience
9	owed, valuable, emerald, diamond rained/reigned
10	probably, afford, interest, holiday, services, decide, insurance, loans current/currant
11	careful, realised, pattern, enables, rely, nowadays, pleasant, accidents, occurring, diet, dangerous whole/hole wait/weight
12	minutes, necessary, business, committee, occasionally omitted, altered, secretary, arguments, resolution, importance, ensure past/passed paw/poor/pore/pour discussed/disgust
13	enquiring, furniture, information, utensils, addresses addition/edition
14	tourist, fields, routes, brief, interrupted practice/practise quiet/quite flour/flower
15	major, policy, subscription, increased, facilities, delayed, interview, appointment

16	allowance, percentage, wholesaler, retailer, encourage, bulk, approval, invoice, official, system, allotted, spreads, carriage, promptly
17-22	annual, concerned, renovation, crescent, appreciated, materials, suitable, catalogue, stretch, luxurious, behaviour, reservation, agency, assistant, abrupt, discourage, arrival, receptionist birth/berth
23-28	luncheon, vouchers, issued, handicapped, notify, committee, responsibility, deducted, salary, attend, suggestions, secretarial, applied, applicants, necessary, qualifications, redecoration, anniversary, inconvenience
29-34	urgent, quotation, receipt, possibility, machine, designed, impressed, alternative, partially, queries, appointed, admirably, efficient, colleagues, reference, appreciate, prior, necessitating, allocated, availability, regarding, applicants, accordingly, endeavour, numerous, tenancy, candidate bases/basis
35-39	regular, schedule, flights, arrangements, Giro, software, cells, spreadsheets, data, graphics, database, retrieve affected/effected fairs/fares

AUDIO-TYPEWRITING

RECORD SHEET

Name ....

Group ....

At the end of each section of work and at the end of each lesson complete this record sheet.

Unit	Task	Tape number and side of tape	Point on scale at which you finished typing	Date and your signature	Teacher's signature
1	1				
	2				
	3				
	4				
2	5				
	6 (a)				
	(b)				
	(c)				
	7				
	8				
	9				
3	10				
	11				
	12				
4	13				
	14				
	15 (a)				
	(b)				
	(c)				
	16				
5	17				
	18				
	19				
	20				
	21				
	22				
6	23				
	24				
	25				
	26				
	27				
	28				
7	29				
	30				
	31				
	32				
	33				
	34				
8	35				
	36				
	37				
	38				
	39				